The Surrey With The Fringe On Top

To OKLAHOMA! and my parents on their 50th

JW

SIMON & SCHUSTER BOOKS FOR YOUNG READERS
Simon & Schuster Building, Rockefeller Center, 1230 Avenue of the Americas, New York, New York 10020.
Text copyright © 1943 by Williamson Music. Copyright renewed. International copyright secured. All rights reserved.
Used by permission. Courtesy of the Rodgers and Hammerstein Organization.
Illustrations copyright © 1993 by James Warhola.
All rights reserved including the right of reproduction in whole or in part in any form.
SIMON & SCHUSTER BOOKS FOR YOUNG READERS
is a trademark of Simon & Schuster.
The text of this book is set in 17 point Icone Light 45. The illustrations were done in pen and ink and watercolor.
Manufactured in the United States of America

10 9 8 7 6 5 4 3 2 1

Library of Congress Cataloging-in-Publication Data
Hammerstein, Oscar, 1895-1960. [Surrey with the fringe on top]
Rodgers and Hammerstein's The surrey with the fringe on top / lyrics by Oscar Hammerstein II ; music by Richard Rodgers ;
illustrations by James Warhola. Summary: A nighttime ride in the surrey with the fringe on top is a grand and beautiful experience.
1. Children's songs—Texts.   [1. Songs.]   I. Rodgers, Richard, 1902-   .   II. Warhola, James, ill.
PZ8.3.H1865Ro   1993   782.42163'0268—dc20   CIP   92-2462   ISBN 0-671-79456-6

The lyrics that appear in this book are taken from *Lyrics by Oscar Hammerstein II* © 1949, 1985 by the
Estate of Oscar Hammerstein. Lyrics and music on the endpapers are taken from sheet music for
children © 1956 by Williamson Music, Inc. Consequently spelling variants appear.

RODGERS AND HAMMERSTEIN'S

The Surrey With The Fringe On Top

LYRICS BY OSCAR HAMMERSTEIN II
MUSIC BY RICHARD RODGERS

ILLUSTRATED BY JAMES WARHOLA

SIMON & SCHUSTER BOOKS FOR YOUNG READERS
Published by Simon & Schuster
New York   London   Toronto   Sydney   Tokyo   Singapore

When I take you out tonight with me,
Honey, here's the way it's goin' to be:
You will set behind a team of snow-white horses
In the slickest gig you ever see!

Chicks and ducks and geese better scurry
When I take you out in the surrey,
When I take you out in the surrey with the fringe on top.

Watch thet fringe and see how it flutters
When I drive them high-steppin' strutters—
Nosey-pokes'll peek through their shutters and their eyes
will pop!

The wheels are yeller, the upholstery's brown,
The dashboard's genuine leather,
With isinglass curtains y' c'n roll right down
In case there's a change in the weather;
Two bright side lights winkin' and blinkin',
Ain't no finer rig, I'm a-thinkin';
You c'n keep yer rig if you're thinkin' 'at I'd keer to swap
Fer that shiny little surrey with the fringe on the top.

Would y' say the fringe was made of silk?
Wouldn't have no other kind but silk.
Has it really got a team of snow-white horses?
One's like snow—the other's more like milk.

All the world'll fly in a flurry
When I take you out in the surrey,
When I take you out in the surrey with the fringe on top.
When we hit that road, hell fer leather,
Cats and dogs'll dance in the heather,

Birds and frogs'll sing all together, and the toads will hop!

The wind'll whistle as we rattle along,
The cows'll moo in the clover,
The river will ripple out a whispered song,
And whisper it over and over:
Don't you wisht y'd go on ferever?
Don't you wisht y'd go on ferever?
Don't you wisht y'd go on ferever and ud never stop
In that shiny little surrey with the fringe on the top?

I can see the stars gittin' blurry
When we ride back home in the surrey,
Ridin' slowly home in the surrey with the fringe on top.
I can feel the day gittin' older,
Feel a sleepy head near my shoulder,
Noddin', droopin' close to my shoulder till it falls, kerplop!

The sun is swimmin' on the rim of a hill,
The moon is takin' a header,
And jist as I'm thinkin' all the earth is still,
A lark'll wake up in the medder...
Hush! You bird, my baby's a-sleepin'—
Maybe got a dream worth a-keepin'.

Whoa! You team, and jist keep a-creepin'
       at a slow clip-clop;
Don't you hurry with the surrey with the
       fringe on the top.